dreams
through
an
open
window

raymond shaw

nprnt press

First printing December 2012

published by
nprnt press
www.nprntpress.com

ISBN 978-0-9877067-3-7

To
Jessie and Rowan,
without whose love and support
nothing would be possible.

Contents

Foreword

dreams through an open window has been sitting
on a hard drive, unpublished, for over 15 years.
Raymond Shaw began this collection of poetry in 1984,
finishing it in the spring of 1994. In June of that year,
he made it a birthday gift to his partner and sent it
to her while she was travelling in England. The gift
was the first (and until now, only) printed version—a
small, handmade, pocket-sized edition. Later, Shaw
created a web site devoted to the work and a circle
of dedicated supporters developed. The author
now welcomes the decision to publish and thereby
share *dreams through an open window* with a wider
audience.

dreams through an open window forms an
experiment in poetry: individual poems that stand on
their own, but when taken together, create a whole.
Shaw suggests that you read the poems in sequence,
from beginning to end, to receive the full impact
and overall intent of the piece, after which, you may
choose to enjoy the poems as you wish.

Influenced by T.S. Eliot, in terms of his thoughts on artistic development, and Theodore Roethke's view that poetry could act in a similar way to the power of prose, Shaw was inspired to create *dreams through an open window*. His intention is to add his voice to those who are urging the creation of a world where true justice prevails—not just for the privileged few, but for all, regardless of their circumstances. In this new, just world, everyone will have a right to live, not only a life of dignity, but a life where they are accepted for who they are, contributing their unique gift—that gift is themselves; then will we see a true reflection of the diversity of the life we all share: in a phrase, a unity in diversity.

The author hopes that by reading *dreams through an open window* people will experience a glimpse into their own inner self and find a moment of release from their daily challenges. He recommends that you: *"Dip into this collection, when you want to dream of other things."*

છ

"Little Lamb, who made thee?
Dost thou know who made thee?"

—William Blake

Synopsis

In *dreams through an open window,* the author combines the ideas of the poets T.S. Eliot *(in relation to meaning)* and Theodore Roethke *(in relation to form),* as expressed in the quotes below. The collection is a metaphorical journey, following the unfolding of a poetical consciousness from youth to maturity.

The work begins with a statement of poetical principles, which is followed by the renting of a blank page, revealing an emerging verse hidden behind the opaqueness of thought. The journey ends with a revelation which connects the beginning and end of existence; between the two are moments of struggle and joy.

ॐ

"So long as artists exist, making what they please and think they ought to make, even if it is not terribly good, even if it appeals to only a handful of people, they remind the Management of something managers need to be reminded of, namely, that the managed are people with faces, not anonymous members, that Homo Laborans *is also* Homo Ludens.*"* —W.H. Auden

"*The progress of an artist is a continual self-sacrifice, a continual extinction of personality.*" —T.S. Eliot

"*Miracles are to come. With you I leave a remembrance of miracles: they are by somebody who can love and who shall be continually reborn, a human being; somebody who said to those near him, when his fingers would no longer hold a brush 'tie it into my hand.' *" —e.e. cummings

"*Like a piece of ice on a hot stove the poem must ride on its own melting.*" —Robert Frost

"*The secrets of individual imagination—which are transconceptual & non-verbal—I mean unconditioned Spirit—are not for sale to this consciousness, are of no use to this world, except perhaps to make it shut its trap & listen to the music of the Spheres.*"
—Allen Ginsberg

"*We must permit poetry to extend consciousness as far, as deeply, as particularly as it can, to recapture, in Stanley Kunitz's phrase, what it has lost to some extent to prose.*" —Theodore Roethke

৪০

Statement of Poetical Principles

The age of science as we know it is at an end. Science, with its current form and methods of exploration of the phenomenal world, has taken humanity almost as far as it possibly can in its search for the meaning of life. The fruit of scientific endeavour has enabled us to discover how many things work in our cosmos, however, bound as it is to the tangible world, science has discovered only the how of cosmos, not the why.

Now begins the age of the human being.

We know many of the Laws, but not from where they come; such a result is not so unusual. The life that demonstrates through the cosmos is beyond the form, as are we; the mystic and the poet know this to be true. This intangible aspect, to which we ascribe the collective name God, exists beyond the mind.

The mind, however, seeks to limit this boundless expression we call God to a mental concept that is explainable and consistent with science's Godless view; however, this is impossible.

Now begins the age of the human being. We will continue to use the findings of science in our lives, but its role as the arbiter of reality is over. Just as in the Romantic period in literature two hundred years ago, the human spirit rises to the surface once more, demanding expression for the inexpressible, not in chaotic clashes of rhyme, indicative of uncertain times, or in strident expostulations, so prevalent in recent poetry. The passing of these forms is a sign that the birthing season is over and a new time is here. The keynote of the new time is joy—the joy of life, which establishes right relationships. We *are* the answer to the question of the millennium. We *are* the marriage of heaven and hell, come to give witness to the bounty we call love.

The poesy of the new time requires a range of imagery that reflects the inexpressible experience of life, while at the same time, demonstrating that life in the world around us. The first logical choice is Nature, as Nature embodies the unknowable aspect of God transcendent. This metaphorical assignment encompasses the outward expression of life, but for our purposes, we should augment this with a second aspect to create a compound metaphor that can accommodate the new life which seeks expression.

> *Each poet will be unique, but each will reflect a unity in diversity.*

The second answer, therefore, is the human being's experience in life. The human being represents God immanent and through the interrelationship of the two—the human experience and Nature's demonstrations—the fullest possible expression of God can be given in time and space. Add to this combination the analogy of the dream as representative of shifting consciousness, and we have a mixture that lends itself to poetical expression of the highest level. This new poesy will reflect the poet's personal experience as stimulated and inspired by Nature, which the writer will then express in ordered words of invocative meaning. The resultant poetical styles will, in turn, stimulate similar revelations in like-minded individuals for a flowering of creative offerings unknown in human history.

The new poetical expression must not be didactic, seeking to assert one view or experience over another. Rather, it must be expressive of the life we have, observe, intuit, and experience. The words should come from an overflowing of joy that cannot be contained. The poet will have to work in a frenzy of activity to capture the moment of exaltation, then apply a talent for sound, order, and beauty to create a poem fit for the annals of high art.

High art has a long history in humanity's sojourn on this earth, and we must build from its foundations to erect the new edifice of poetical art. Of all the arts, the written word, especially poetry, is the most powerful and the most difficult to fully understand.

Nevertheless, it is incumbent upon those drawn
to poetry to record their thoughts, feelings and
expressions, with the hope that those who can, will
understand their writings.

Today's poet is charged with a challenging
task, but one which must be taken up gladly and
with joy. The communion with the inner and outer
realities will liberate the poet, revealing a life of
right relationships and a life more abundant, in the
fullest sense of the word. This being so, no one poet
can hope to represent the entire scope of life's joy.
Only through a collection of poetical works from
various poets can an approximation of life's fullness
be shown. Each poet will be unique, but each will
reflect a unity in diversity. Poems will sing of life's
joy and life's struggle for expression, accompanied by
an inexpressible quality indicative of that which lies
behind our daily occurrences.

Chaucer began this tradition of poetical concern
with a greater life, using a stylistic device of viewing
the world through the poet's eyes. Milton sought to
express "the ways of God to man" in a framework

that moved our view from a remote heaven to man in the world, as God's creation, tinged with humanistic views. Shakespeare brought us closer to today's views with his joyous sonnets that celebrate life and seek to illustrate to fellow human beings the life that lies dormant in so many. Wordsworth, Coleridge, Shelley, and especially Blake, exploded the form of poetry, taking it into a wonderland of human potential and greatness.

The conflicts and uncertainties of the present [20th] century of transition have affected many poets, who reflect this inner and outer conflict in their poetry. Now, at last, the times begin to be conducive to a resurgence of poetical beauty and stylistic rhythm and meter befitting high art.

> *The call goes forth for poets to rise to the opportunity of the time.*

The leveling of society that has taken place during the past century has helped to create the means for this new development in poetry. However, a devastating side effect has been a reduction in artistic expression to a lowest-common-denominator mediocrity and this must be rectified through a concerted effort to fulfill humanity's highest aspirations. Only in this way can visions be seen and vistas of imaginings explored. Continuing to be preoccupied with pleasing those who wish simply to consume the latest "product" will doom poetry to become nothing more than a disposable commodity, no different from the most banal advertising, and we cannot allow this to happen. Just as the new wine deserves new bottles, so too, the new poesy demands new forms and levels of imagining.

So, with high aspirations and armed with a sensitivity to life's love coursing through humanity's veins, the poet is charged to take up the written word for the glorification of life's beauty. This love and beauty are qualities that stem from the highest source—the source of life itself. The name we choose

for the source matters not—call it the Godhead,
the higher self, the Self, the soul; all are imperfect
terms for a truth which we each know unconsciously,
but suspect to be true, and to which we owe our
existence, and which can only be experienced, not
housed within thought. The poet must help others to
experience the life that lies hidden at the heart of all,
and point the way for others to follow.

Thus, with great expectations and humble words,
is this statement of poetical principles offered. The
call goes forth for poets to rise to the opportunity of
the time. No greater service could there be than for
poets to discover themselves and to commit to the
written word their experiences for others to share.
For, in that sharing, the unity of life will be sensed,
known, and realized. This unity, in turn, will reveal
ourselves to each other as God.

—R.M. Shaw
May 1994

This Night

A
mom
ent of li
ght, this night
passes into my hear
t to view, as withered w
ings of ancient days collap
se amid ruins of lost purple's d
ark due, and soul-battered, bruised t
ime slips through my fingers, wet with ye
sterday's sun, while our empty womb cries wor
d-sunk in birth, unseen by stilled-life v
ision, tombed by blackened wall now c
racked, this night by first light,
soft on wings from out the e
ast, promise-laden come t
o sit easy in shared
garden, the fruit,
a gift of he
arts com
plet
e

Paradise Next

Beside you, crushed,
lest the owner forget, one is sent
to see sunrise rise
in Paradise
next.

Bubbling tears condemn
all ways forgot;
and tears are fears
to ways, and ways you see,
of Paradise
next.

Sing in quarters,
voice of Godless souls;
work, work onwards
in fogs; then onward, onward, yet,
to Paradise
next.

March endlessly
no-wards in quest
denied and lost,
while love is yours to hold and behold
here below,
in Paradise
next.

The Dream is Alive!

In the corridors of industry and commerce,
humanity lies dormant and raging,
tied to waste and indolent behaviour,
amidst sleepless sessions and endless cycles
of cheque book debits
and thin lines of sleeping credit.

Money-tired, monkey-minded men
fill shops, factories and malls with
wandering children, caught in life by rote,
and one by one, all pass
to graveyards filled with empty lives.

In a window-seat, sits a child
playing in clouds of sea-washed white
amidst night-castles of wayward winds,
as
mommy's medicine plays against the day
and daddy brings home tomorrow's news
in a cellophane-wrapped basket of farewell fruit.

Dreams play upon dreams,
curving under man's bleak, black board,
carrying the child wayward and homeward,
away from the dead and
away from the end,
back home, back to the dream.

For, despite weight delivered
—by profit, indolence and time—
the dream is alive!
the dream is alive!
soaring through mind after mind,
through all humankind,
unbeknownst to headlines parceled with
dour fear—
in all sudden acts of rhyme;
the dream is alive!
the dream is alive!

Tortoise-green mountains blaze
with dawn of dusty rose,
amidst pining children who sit in window-seats,
idle of commerce,
fond of secrets, alive to dreams,
immune to purulent greed.

Yes, 'tis true—
while the many sleep a stupored sleep,
the dream is alive!
the dream is alive!

An End

"Two times the sun plus six,"
the little one said.
"Thirty-two Jupiters and a moon,"
the other said.
"One source of creation,"
the third one said.
And the game was automatically over.

In Glen Down Wood

In Glen Down Wood
branches bow,
brittle under winter's hoary breath,
and makeshift castles shift their sights,
not to the east,
nor to first night's light.
Winter blows
in Glen Down Wood,
and all is buried underground—
life is still,
except for sound
of crunching snow
and tiny birds—
watching!

In Glen Down Wood,
white-scaped, smooth and gentle rest
blankets tomorrow's turbid mirage,
and all is still,
my silent reader,
all is still
in Glen Down Wood.

You, silent reader,
of Ages and no name,
read, in silent time,
this coddling-chaste scene,

which some writers write on
as if still-life-left night,
and know it for that sweet sleep
where mornings pass into mornings,
all the hours to keep.

All is quiet
in Glen Down Wood,
residence of the still,
homeland to those who pass unseen,
awaiting anew
the sojourn you bring.

Linger awhile
in Glen Down Wood;
touch green grass rolling time
and see the life that so many miss,
openly
blanketed
here.

This Is My Love

Grey-bearded man,
who will one day stand
at the portal of my future,
read the verse of which I sang first,
from green days of unripened line,
cast in a crooked house
with pink falling rhododendrons facing north:

"My love on descending stairs—
stray calico cat, hairless back legs, sad,
cradled soft in inviting lap, the afternoon May day
sun, cool, bright upon fair hair—
sitting still, thinking in red
and multicoloured stripes—
this is my love."

Old man, to whom I turn,
I am young and love knows me;
no more may I write,
for love draws me hard
to her wisdom, beauty and light,
and if life be anything so sweet
as this time with her,
then I shall never weep, nor sleep more.

That Grey Land

I live in that grey land
between waking
and sleeping,
where dreams are best
kept secret
and lives are never lived,
except in memories of lost lust
and painful remorse.

My dead dreams
see no justice, no freedom;
no longer are my eyes for seeing,
only for weeping and
sleeping through memory
of life lived in a grey desert
with no sun, no horizon;
no longer life,
only a thin, thin line of grey,
kept in a half-kept window.

Indictment

A fresh, young child lies bloated
upon the broken, brown ground,
her taut, grotesque stomach full round,
gorged with gurgling emptiness,
dirty, black, filthy flies walking bold
upon her open, sightless eyes.
There lies our shame,
our wretchedness,
our greed,
our deed.

She has not seen three and sees no more,
as near her mother she lies,
limbs the size of bones, eyes glazed,
denied any true action from you or me.

Out of the mouths of tens of millions
we stole our bounty,
wasted, usurped, and dismissed all,
with no remorse
and no recourse for homeless,
starving millions;
yet—
that child
is my child,
is our child,
is your child.

Look, and see the deed:
the young,
the sick,
the elderly,
the able-bodied of our world
dying for lack of food;
the ample food which lies rotting
in the store-houses of our world;
food the world gave willingly;
food which separates all from life,
from death.

For how long can we do this?
For how long?

Plumb deep inside yourself
and seek the common thread that binds us all,
and remember your actions,
your deeds,
your part,
and read with shame,
with pain,
this blasphemy,
this writ,
this passing,
this record of our—
indictment.

The Birds' Song

Birds have sung,
once,
twice,
thrice,
in ears that seldom hear—
though not for them do they sing,
these copper-voiced ones—
singing free,
amidst God's
bounteous seed.
These heralds
bob and dive,
dodging man's grasp
in fast-rising morning's tide,
riding high on waves bringing
fresh the dawn,
above man's churlish
line of sorrowful lies.
The evening,
thick-black,
stills the song;
while complete, 'tis not complete;
for others fill the sky,
when stars touch the earth
and nightingales sing with gulls and owls,
till, once again, we see
mother's mornings'-Son's-tide rise.

Sorry,
cast-down man
runs deaf-dumb, blind, naked,
seeking lost laureates
amidst rivers
of singular praise
from those long shadows, long forgotten,
and long earth-bound gone—
death is the only constant companion,
reminder for sorry,
clay-fleshed man.
Song is the birds' gift,
derived from a sweet refrain—never, never
gathered of man's rhythm, dicta or
earthy, earth-worn rage.
Ears, draw near
to the birds' song
in this design divine—
seek the union that hides, discreet and complete,
—come listen awhile
to these of heaven, wind and fire.
Yes, birds have sung
in ears that seldom hear,
once,
twice,
thrice.

In Dreams They Sail

Sea-breath sting
brings night to clatrian screams,
singing
drop,
drop,
drop
over side,
long-heckled doubt,
companion and slave,
down,
down,
down
into water's cave,
to hold the robe of Jonah,
lost in mired hope amidst the damp
morning's sickly sea air.

Hold and roll with wind's scent
this morning
that quashes all songs' deeds,
for as tales told,
this day shan't pass
'till all the sea shall hold
again
a sailor, once more
sent of quay and chance.

Dream of mast set
with pulling gale,
winds sending rope,
captain, mate and fate,
journeying past all mortal shape,
through brine that yields no sign
of toiling,
deep,
deep,
deep,
over the side,
while on the water's edge
waits,
waits,
waits
love and fruit
for the long-gone Johnnys that
sleep,
sleep,
sleep
in a long-dead, lonely stupor
of Earth-lost
sleep.

Love Lies Naked With Me

Love lies naked with me,
breast upon breast,
hand upon hip,
divorced of lust
and descending in ordered time,
remembering only
a moment passed,
sifted in the sowing of seeds,
graced with gold,
set in silver waves,
soft upon the shores,
pillows for my head,
heavy with day's sleep,
but returning always
to ceaseless yearnings
of comfort that lies there,
deep within your being,
warm and hot,
retiring of thought;
but betwixt us,
naught can wane,
for in your arms
rests my life,
and this to you I give,
never questioning,
always receiving,
morning after morning,

rising after rising;
relentlessly,
my love
of no bounds,
willfully tugs me higher,
to mountain tops,
through caves
of resplendent light
with darkness,
the darkness
left broken
upon still, dusty ground,
mixed in murky water,
bitter to taste;
life emerges,
fused soft betwixt us,
breast to breast,
no you,
no me,
rien ne va plus;
break,
part,
wait,
return,
cycling
time within time,
both ending and beginning,

my love,
naked
with you,
with me,
with all,
with soul-fired,
passionless,
dead desire,
tied to the heart of sorrows,
glad of
you,
relieved of
you,
caught in ascent,
believed in sight,
all in all,
through raising after raising,
falling after falling,
this veil is upon us,
beneath which we stand,
naked,
on view to all;
some take,
some view,
some rise,
drinking it down,
expurgating upon the end,
tired,

defenseless to life,
the fire that burns,
the magnet that holds fast,
seldom revealed,
seldom recognized,
though ashes be heaped upon ashes
and time turned upon herself;
my love,
your love
lies naked
with me.

Overcome by a Dream

Last night I slept,
overcome by a dream.
From within that dream
a great note sounded with a mighty shout,
and you were there.
In darkness, an outstretched hand pulled back
the haughty veil of complacency,
and numbed and unclothed,
we wept,
for before us,
humanity cried, tied to the earth,
robbed of dignity, steeped in fear,
silenced by slavery,
broken of misuse.
We turned with blackened shame
to our mute revealer,
as fellow human beings fell,
crushed under weight of avarice,
hate, jealousy, and ignorance.
From within the dream,
a light, pure, warm, akin to a rose,
released a balm which fired the lust of
freedom and justice unfound, and found, denied.
The single hand pointed into the fog of
humanity's world,
a trumpet sounded with a million million voices,
the people rose up

and cried:
return to your places!
return to your homes!
no rest till all is made right,
no rest till journey's end!
The hand returned us home,
touched our sleeping hearts;
all rushed in, while we rode out the night.
It was said, we heard it all,
yes, you and I heard it all,
as we slept.
It was the song of the one note.
It was the song known as the Call.
Last night, you were there, as was I,
overcome by a dream.

The Sea

We went down to the
sea today
and saw
the sea,
gulls
and ships.

Water was gentle at
the edge
and it
moved
like movie stars,
resting between each other's
hips.

Love was a constant line
in our moment of sweet
release,
while couples walked,
gentle today—
down by,
down by
the sea.

Spring

Spring fastens molten time to her wheel,
as dawn of milky white
rocks hard this coal-black me,
'neath sands, blistering-bold-jackal-laugh tight,
and bound and crowned,
I stir, deep behind clay-fleshed words,
while boatmen sleep on distant,
pass-not shores, bone-empty crowded,
awaiting lost season's round to retire the day
the thin-voiced Sibyl set to flight.

Spring's fiat, gull-white against love-blue sky,
carries promises kept silent of my
shaded, sad fool, drunk of reason,
caught fast in late tears of wed-dead, purged,
stoic wordings, playing slippery amidst acts of time,
numbered in every leaf and blade of grass that ever
was or ever will be by Sibyl's word heard:
now, see the sweet whisperings' work,
turning all in all upon the cross, north to south
and back again, rent from top to bottom,
the gentle hand stretched still upon the waters.

I step and descend, and turn and rise,
carrying my chains of sorrows,
lost in dumb memory of etched, dim past,
my small voice reaching, now,

out from dark-cast-night,
soul-light-laid-low home,
relaying a love-song long stilled by
mantel's grave-rich pull,
now rising high on wind's breath,
thrilling through most emerald glade and saffron day,
heralding the clarion call of life itself
to shift and move,
removed from grip of nature's tomb.

Remember?

Under an empty afternoon sky of stolen time
youthful solitude does reside,
pale, relaxed and asleep,
sleeping the slow, deep sleep
on which dreamers rely,
wrapped in Mother Earth,
supple and blind green golden,
as tearful embers fall, cast off,
as in an evening's tide—
remember?
Smooth me down and drink long, Father Time,
yet I will not be denied,
for youthful solitude is mine,
under an empty afternoon sky of stolen time.

Saturn's Sad Day

Still voices rage
while winds plague
wild words within
Saturn's sad day.
Today's dreams have all played
and left their mysteries
dead.
*And where are the songs
sung of thee?*—left
green and still
among the morning.

A Day in Sun

A morning dream was dreamed
of Sunday, cream, strawberries,
anemones, baby's breath,
freesias and ferns.

Sun-white day, golden cross 'neath
twilight Seine dream,
dreamed of Sunday mornings' delight—
you, me, hand on hip, breast to breast,
divorced of lust
and descending in ordered time.

Dream a dream, when sleep is steeped in
sinking afternoon and noon is fresh behind
the sun-potted memory that brought sweet juice of
Eros, Pan, Venus and Albion warmth,
bed and red, red time.

In Worried Fashion

Widow-wearied, streaked
spring sits still and wet,
as morning turns to afternoon,
in worried fashion.
By leave of leaves, we watched the change
from life to sleep,
and all the thoughts remained,
tossed together,
in worried fashion.
The sleep was long-lived by mute and stone,
and all day caught
in worried fashion, by chance,
in a muddled dream. We hastened
to destiny,
our only fashion,
agreed of deeds and thieves
and sun-lost beliefs.
Green evening waits still-born in time,
breathing broken songs
of heaving day—
alone—
as we tumble down
the life we sought,
caught
in worried fashion.

The Way

I touched the silver side of the green mountain
and stood, proud, upon the shore of my sea,
when winds beat about the season's moan.
I emptied my conscience,
and was tempted like Eve, Job, Christ;
fallen, I ate apples of ash,
as harpies sang the ancient lament
of light as darkness,
and voices talked the justification of God's ways to
man by means of compurgation.
In the doing, I huddled near my fire
and sank in an ocean of read words,
worked to red death and stuck in my fall;
my fall, set in a dream,
ran in molten footprints,
in wet sand, between waves,
impressed existence caused by weight of presence,
set in a moment,
reflective to destined dissolve,
when a hand stills the waters,
and yet another wave appears.
The child's eyes cried to me
and I stood,
and I listened;
the wave was as a sentinel,
showing the way,
and I understood.

There Is No Dream Today

There is no dream today,
only "I."
I do not ache.
I do not feel.
I do not think.

There is no dream today,
there is only "I,"
a red sparrow in an angelic host returned.
I see.
I know.
I act.
I am as the tree upon the sand,
upon the beach, turned to glass.

There is no dream today,
only "I,"
the shadow puppet in the black,
turned to ash,
without that angel from o'er the east gate,
prostrate to adamantine rock,
bouncing to the tree.

My memory makes the dream,
but I am as the sea's seeds without end,
and there is no dream today,
only "I."

The Reflection

The still pool bears my resemblance.
There is my beauty,
my dilemma,
for yet, I cannot see myself.

A blaze of glory overshadows me,
while another blots out my image,
holding me fast in a grip of Ages,
white-hot with fierce desire choking my way,
pushing me from the water's edge,
denying me my wedding day.

Slip loose these tight knots;
let me glide free from my captor
who pulls the oar of
that solitary boat,
bound for shores
of stilled life of
restless boredom.

After the wake and during the sleep,
time keeps me and harbours me;
naught that I do is done
because of reflective delight.
My pool is as a cauldron,
tossed down to seek another,
the twin that gazes at me.

The ring that holds the water burns bright;
a balm of peace blesses its stillness
and looks for my face.
My fingers disturb the surfaces.
My limbs defile its graces.
Still you seek me to fill your need,
and here, I!

The reflection is imperfect during this night.
Come light, take the sight and put it to your use,
that I may see myself in the still pool
and know beauty in the world.

This Rainbow

My love departs
and the world is wound down.
The lustre leaves the laburnum,
its heavy blooms shot through with sulphur yellow.
Sighs and tears replace my clear eyes' sight;
rain from cloudless skies
pours into my heart that near breaks
at thought of time without you.

Love, where is your grace
that lifts my foot upon the path
and smooths my way?

The sun is put out.
Chaos is come to the universe.
The steady sea is amok with torment.
Indigo sky sinks to boot-black dye.

Where is your smile, my love?
Gone—
and I am alone.

'Tis true, the few knew you,
but I knew you best and was blest.
I say, "The world has seen none as you!"
And I wait my life to see you again.

Night be gone!
Morn, turn up your light to light my world.
My love returns anon on wings of glory,
amidst streams of golden rays;
the arc of my covenant,
I am less than half without you
and more than whole with.
Pass my way again, my love,
and never let's part again.

Dreams Through An Open Window

There was a time,
but it is over,
when a pleasure-dome was decreed,
and living legend passéd life,
and emerald grass was made
for angels to dance upon;
rhyme ran like the river Alph,
and hollowed words had not been formed;
contemplation sank the land,
then the arm of the night shaded the world,
and the dream set in.

Water tumbled into the deep,
splitting the adamantine rock in two,
creating life where there had been none.
The light violated the night,
bringing the life to song;
a birthing began that begat the wind,
soft on a brow of cloudless blue.

A scribe scribbled a note,
sent to see a morning rise in rage.
A voice asked, *"Where are we to go?"*
"Below," was a single reply,
"Not to worry, or to cry;"
a ring was passed to seal the scene.

The dreamer awoke.
Light lit up the leaves;
sinewy lines ran a course,
bridging the moment between waking and sleep,
and red mingled with the green,
bringing shape to form to life to death to life.

A chain was forged, linking a wheel within a wheel;
a howl rose up and a voice asked,
"Where are we to go?"
"Above," was a single reply.
Through the worry, with the tears,
the ring was pierced to finish the scene.

My vision saw in and out in a moment;
tears evaporated in mists of love;
a cup of sorrows was lifted to my lips;
soft waters flowed into my heart.

The remaining rainbow glittered
with words of May trees and Wisteria;
a stream sang her song to us,
as goldfinches sat upon the bough,
a crystal pool below our feet;
the pleasure-dome was but a memory
that sank like the land,
all those centuries ago.

An ancient voice
welcomed all home;
within the circle,
all had come to witness a holy moment,
as the Rod was wielded,
held high above the heads of the crowd.

The sun touched the Diamond
and all fell upon their knees;
a song arose with the morn
that brought me here
to write of the parting of a dream;
that brought me here to write,
as one who saw
dreams through an open window.

finis

About the author

Raymond Shaw was born in British Columbia, Canada in the spring of 1953. He displayed a creative nature at an early age, taking up music and composition, and later turning to writing and poetry. In 1988 he became a freelance graphic designer, and after a few years, now with a background in art history, he started researching the techniques of painting. With a growing urge to explore oil painting, he finally bought paints and brushes and began to paint.

As an artist, he is concerned with unity and the hope to see it demonstrate through humanity. He suggests that unity is only possible when true justice exists for all; justice is only possible when we have trust, which, in turn, will only be present when we learn to see humanity as one family, and when we adopt the principle of sharing as the basis for our relationships.

Raymond Shaw lives in Burnaby, Canada with his partner of 36 years, their son, and Leo the cat. Please visit his website, **raymondshaw.ca** to view his paintings.

Cover illustration: Emerging World II

Painted by Raymond Shaw, *Emerging World II* (oil on canvas; 28" x 22" / 71.12 cm x 55.88 cm) is one in a series. The artist describes his painting as follows:

"Emerging World II is a painting that tries to depict the world that is coming into being, that is emerging out of this world and is not yet defined; that's why this picture is somewhat ambiguous. We have a blue sphere, either coming into the picture or going out of the picture, and down in the right is a red circle, which is either a new world emerging there or an influence, possibly. The other colours around represent divinity, at one level or another, or the physical world, in one way or another."